All the Answers
(AND MUCH MUCH MORE)

Published in Great Britain in 2014 by Canongate Books Ltd,
14 High Street, Edinburgh EH1 1TE

www.canongate.tv

1

British Library Cataloguing-in-Publication Data
A catalogue record for this book is available on
request from the British Library

ISBN 978 1 78211 311 9
Paperback ISBN 978 1 78211 550 2

PEANUTS written and drawn by Charles M. Schulz
Edited by Andy Miller and Jenny Lord
Design: Rafaela Romaya
Layout: Stuart Polson

CHARLES M. SCHULZ

LIFE LESSONS FROM
LUCY

CANONGATE
Edinburgh · London

BEAN BAGS ARE A BOON TO SULKERS

HOW'S THIS? IS THIS ANY BETTER?
MUCH BETTER.. VERY EFFECTIVE

GOOD
CRABBY LOOKS TAKE A LOT OF PRACTICE

YOU KNOW WHAT SURPRISES ME?
I'M SURPRISED THAT YOU DIDN'T FALL IN LOVE WITH ME THE VERY FIRST TIME YOU SAW ME...
LIFE IS FULL OF SURPRISES

I CAN UNDERSTAND HOW YOU MIGHT BECOME INFATUATED WITH ME
ONE THING I WOULDN'T WANT YOU TO DO, HOWEVER, AND THAT WOULD BE TO PUT ME ON A PEDESTAL
GOOD!
WUMP!
OF COURSE, IF I WERE ON A PEDESTAL, I COULD REALLY RUN THINGS

I THINK I'D LIKE TO TAKE PIANO LESSONS
WOULDN'T YOU LIKE TO GIVE ME PIANO LESSONS?

WE COULD SIT SIDE BY SIDE
I THINK I'LL SWITCH TO THE VIOLIN

IF SOMEONE CLOSE TO YOU NOTICED THAT YOU HAD SOME FAULTS, WOULD YOU WANT THEM POINTED OUT TO YOU?
WELL, SURE..I GUESS SO..

THEN, HERE WE GO!

I DON'T **HAVE** TO LIVE IN THIS HOUSE, YOU KNOW!
I CAN FIND MY OWN APARTMENT, AND LIVE BY MYSELF!
TEN YEARS FROM NOW!

ALL RIGHT, IF EVERYONE IN THIS HOUSE HATES ME SO MUCH, I'LL JUST LEAVE!!
THAT'LL MAKE YOU ALL HAPPY, WON'T IT?
WHY SHOULD I MAKE THEM ALL HAPPY?

LUCY, YOU'RE THE WORST PLAYER WE HAVE! YOU'RE HOPELESS! YOU'RE NO HELP TO US AT ALL!!!

I LOOKED GOOD IN THE TEAM PICTURE

PSYCHIATRIC HELP 34¢
THE DOCTOR IS IN
YOU SAY I'M HOPELESS
WOULD IT BOTHER YOU IF I ASKED FOR A SECOND OPINION ?

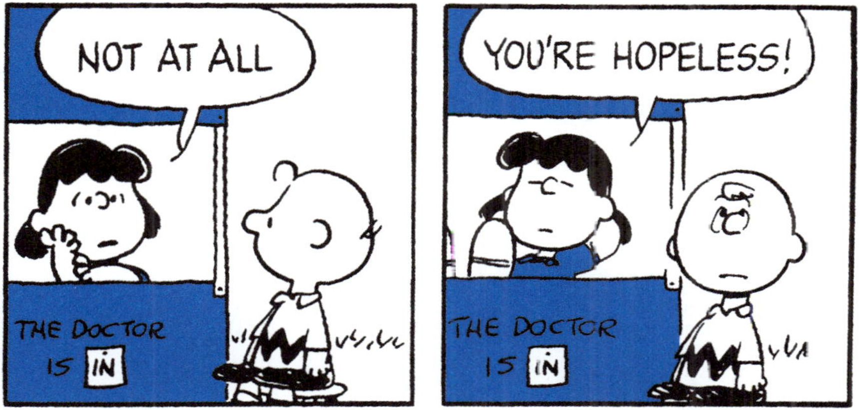
NOT AT ALL
THE DOCTOR IS IN
YOU'RE HOPELESS!
THE DOCTOR IS IN

I HEARD SOMEONE ON TV SAY THAT THE WORLD IS GETTING WORSE EVERY DAY
THAT'S RIDICULOUS!
HOW COULD THE WORLD BE GETTING WORSE WITH ME IN IT? EVER SINCE I WAS BORN THE WORLD HAS SHOWN A DISTINCT IMPROVEMENT!
I MAKE THE WORLD BETTER! I'M A POSITIVE FORCE!

SMILE!
SEE? WITH ME AROUND, EVERYONE IS A LOT HAPPIER!

BY THE TIME I'VE GROWN UP, WE'LL PROBABLY HAVE A WOMAN PRESIDENT..
YOU KNOW WHAT THAT MEANS, DON'T YOU?

IT MEANS I WON'T GET TO BE THE FIRST ONE...
BOY, THAT MAKES ME MAD!!

AS SOON AS THIS GROUND IS SPADED, I'M GOING TO ORGANIZE MY GARDEN
I'M GOING TO PLANT POTATOES, AND BEANS, AND RADISHES AND PEAS

WHY ARE YOU TELLING ME ALL THIS?
OH!

HERE'S THE WORLD FAMOUS DIVER ABOUT TO PERFORM HIS FANTASTIC FORWARD RUNNING DIVE...
DON'T YOU DARE!
FOLLOWED BY HIS "KEEP GOING AND PROBABLY LAND ON HIS HEAD" DIVE!

HERE COMES THE FANTASTIC FORWARD RUNNING DIVE...
OH, NO YOU DON'T!
FOLLOWED BY THE FANTASTIC MIDAIR TURNAROUND!

STAY RIGHT WHERE YOU ARE, OR I'LL POUND YOU!
THIS IS GOING TO BE HARD TO DO...

SORRY, DOG.. NO MORE AIR.. NO MORE WATER..
BUT LOTS OF GROUND...

IT'S VERY STRANGE...
IT HAPPENS JUST BY LOOKING AT YOU

WHAT HAPPENS ?
I CAN FEEL A CRITICISM COMING ON

BONK!
AAUGH!
LUCY! HOW COULD YOU MISS THAT BALL?! IT CAME RIGHT TO YOU! HOW COULD YOU MISS IT?!!
I NEVER THINK ABOUT THE PAST

WE'RE NEVER GONNA WIN A GAME!
WE'RE GONNA LOSE EVERY GAME WE PLAY FOR THE REST OF OUR LIVES!
BONK!
SORRY, MANAGER.. THE FUTURE GOT IN MY EYES!

LOST AGAIN! I CAN'T STAND IT!

WHY? WHY? WHY?

BECAUSE WE'RE NO GOOD... BECAUSE WE'RE NO GOOD... BECAUSE WE'RE NO GOOD!

ALL MY LIFE I WANTED TO BE AN ONLY CHILD... I HAD A GOOD THING GOING 'TIL YOU CAME..
LITTLE BROTHERS SPOIL EVERYTHING..LITTLE BROTHERS ARE A BOTHER AND A NUISANCE...

WHY ARE YOU TELLING ME ALL THIS?
THERE'S NOTHING GOOD ON TV!

IN A GOOD CONVERSATION, ONE PERSON TALKS WHILE THE OTHER LISTENS
THEN THAT PERSON TALKS WHILE THE FIRST PERSON LISTENS...
I LIKE TALKING.. I HATE LISTENING
I REALIZE THAT
WHAT ?

RATS...

SULKING IS SPOILED WHEN YOU CAN'T GET COMFORTABLE

DO YOU THINK YOU'RE A DIFFERENT PERSON FROM WHAT YOU WERE LAST YEAR ?
DO YOU THINK YOU'VE REALLY CHANGED?
I REMEMBER LAST YEAR YOU SAID YOU WERE GOING TO TRY TO BE A BETTER LISTENER..
WHAT ?

IT SAYS HERE THAT THE WORLD REVOLVES AROUND THE SUN ONCE A YEAR..
THE WORLD REVOLVES AROUND THE SUN?
ARE YOU SURE?
I THOUGHT IT REVOLVED AROUND ME!

WHO SAYS I'M CRABBY?

SNOWPERSON!

Dear Santa Claus,
I know you will be getting lots of letters this month.
I am writing now so I can be the first one.

I MAILED MINE YESTERDAY

I CAN'T HELP THINKING THAT THIS WOULD BE A BETTER WORLD IF EVERYONE WOULD LISTEN TO ME..
MAYBE WE COULD ARRANGE IT...

TRY TO GET THEM ALL IN ONE ROOM..I HATE TO SAY THINGS TWICE..

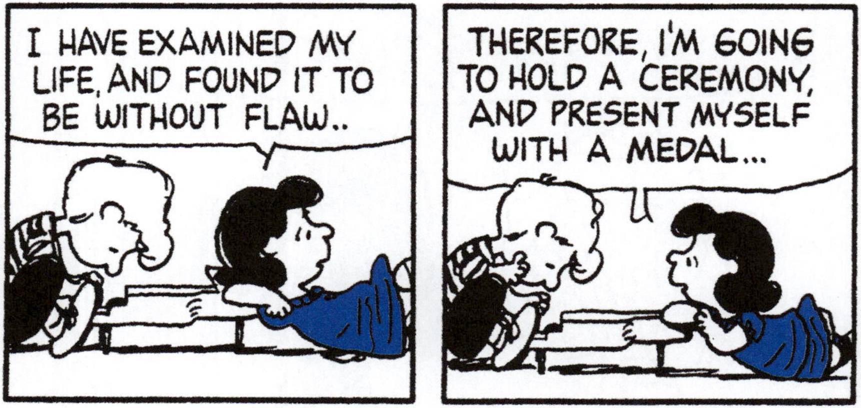
I HAVE EXAMINED MY LIFE, AND FOUND IT TO BE WITHOUT FLAW..
THEREFORE, I'M GOING TO HOLD A CEREMONY, AND PRESENT MYSELF WITH A MEDAL...

I WILL THEN GIVE A VERY MOVING ACCEPTANCE SPEECH..AFTER THAT, I'LL GREET MYSELF IN THE RECEIVING LINE..
WHEN YOU'RE PERFECT, YOU HAVE TO DO EVERYTHING YOURSELF!

PSYCHIATRIC HELP 5¢
THE DOCTOR IS IN
I'M DEPRESSED AGAIN..
HERE, LET ME HOLD YOUR HAND..
THE DOCTOR

THERE'S THE PROBLEM..
WHAT'S WRONG WITH MY HAND?
IT'S SUPPOSED TO HAVE FIVE CENTS IN IT!
THE DOCTOR IS IN

DO YOU HONESTLY THINK THAT JUST BECAUSE I'M YOUR OLDER SISTER, I ACTUALLY ENJOY TELLING YOU WHAT TO DO?
DO YOU REALLY THINK I ENJOY IT?
YES

HOW DID YOU KNOW?

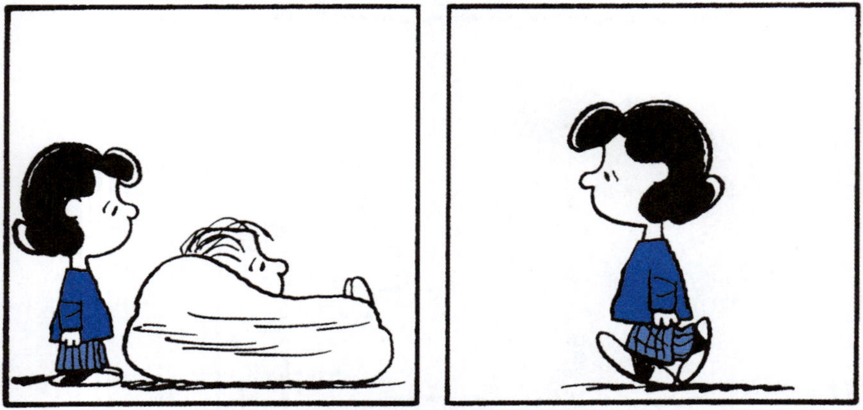

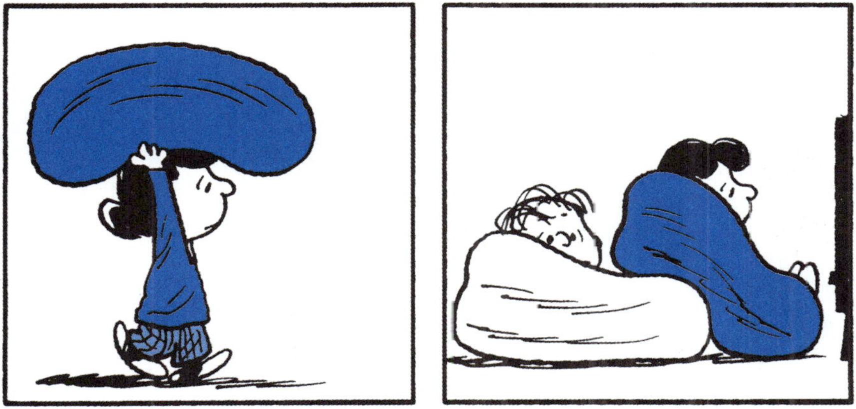

LET'S HAVE A GRUDGE MATCH..
AT WHAT?

I DON'T CARE.. ANYTHING...
I JUST LIKE GRUDGE MATCHES

SURE, THAT'S RIGHT! JUST WALK OUT OF THE ROOM!

YOU KNOW WHAT YOUR TROUBLE IS?
YOU CAN'T TAKE DESTRUCTIVE CRITICISM!

MY GRANDFATHER THINKS HE'S OVER THE HILL
MY GRANDFATHER THINKS HE'S OVER THE HILL AND AROUND THE BEND

MY GRANDFATHER THINKS HE'S OVER THE HILL, AROUND THE BEND, OUT OF THE SWIM AND ON THE SHELF!
SHE ALWAYS HAS TO WIN

SLAM!
GET OUT OF MY BEAN BAG...I WANT TO SULK
GO SULK IN A DINING ROOM CHAIR

YOU CAN'T SULK IN A DINING ROOM CHAIR!

OKAY, SO YOU'RE MY OLDER SISTER..
THAT DOESN'T MAKE YOU MY BOSS!

YOU WERE NOT PUT HERE ON EARTH TO TELL ME WHAT TO DO!
I WASN'T?

THIS ONE IS KIND OF CUTE..
YES, MA'AM.. I'M LOOKING FOR A CARD TO SEND TO A DOG...
HE'S SUCH A WONDERFUL DOG.. HE'S CUTE, AND SMART, AND FRIENDLY AND NICE...

DO YOU HAVE ANY INSULTING CARDS?

I MISSED SCHOOL YESTERDAY BECAUSE I HAD A COLD...
THERE MUST BE SOMETHING GOING AROUND.. LOTS OF KIDS HAVE BEEN GETTING COLDS...

MINE WAS A LOT WORSE, THOUGH...
WHY?
BECAUSE IT HAPPENED TO ME!

ALL RIGHT, WHO DID IT? COME ON! CONFESS!

WHO INVENTED "THANK YOU" NOTES?!

WHAT'S THE MATTER?
DON'T GO NEAR LUCY TODAY... SHE'S IN ONE OF HER SUPER CRABBY MOODS..

WHAT ARE YOU DOING?
SETTING OUT FLARES!

TWO AND A HALF REVOLUTIONS... I USED TO DO BETTER THAN THAT..

WELL, I GUESS I'LL GO TO BED...
BEFORE I GO, WOULD YOU MIND A BRIEF WORD OF CRITICISM?

YES!
I WAS AFRAID OF THAT
IT'S HARD FOR A CRITICAL PERSON TO GO TO SLEEP IF SHE ISN'T ALLOWED A BRIEF WORD OF CRITICISM

I DID IT MY WAY!